I Had A Sister

by Joanne Parker

Illustrated by Sarah Posey

WHP
Wyatt House Publishing

Mobile, Alabama
www.wyattpublishing.com

Wyatt House books may be ordered through booksellers or by contacting:

WYATT HOUSE PUBLISHING
399 Lakeview Dr. W.
Mobile, Alabama 36695
www.wyattpublishing.com
editor@wyattpublishing.com

Because of the dynamic nature of the Internet, any web address or links contained in this book may have changed since publication and may no longer be valid.

Cover and interior design by: Mark Wyatt

ISBN 13: 978-1-7326049-3-3

Printed in the United States of America

For Patty

I had a sister.
She was smart and kind.
She could run really fast.
She could laugh and make everything better.

We shared a room together.
We played games and dolls and we climbed trees.
We told each other secrets.
And we rolled our eyes at each other when we had to go to bed early.

We shared a room together.
We played games and dolls and we climbed trees.
We told each other secrets.
And we rolled our eyes at each other when we had to go to bed early.

We rode the bus together to school.

We sat in the way, way back of the car on road trips.

We dreamed of being in the Olympics and we danced to music all day.

As we got older, we giggled about boys
and we did each other's hair and nails.

We cuddled up under blankets to watch movies.
And we dreamed of life as grown-ups
and traveling the world.

Condolences
on your
Loss

Then one day an accident happened and now she's gone.

Mom told me she was in heaven and we didn't have to be sad.

Dad told me we could remember the good times we had with her and smile.

Friends who came to visit said she was special and loved.

I miss her.

Everyone was very quiet at the funeral and there was a lot of crying.

I wished she had been there to hold my hand.

Everyone was quiet by her grave and there was a lot of hugging.

I wished heaven would give her back.

I miss her.

I miss eating ice cream with my sister.
I miss having someone to dream with.

I miss having someone to ride
in the way, way back with.

I miss laughing so hard my
sides hurt, or laughing for no
reason at all.

I miss her.

And I need to keep eating ice cream,
because she would.

And I need to keep dancing,
because she would.

And I need to keep dreaming,
because she would.

And I need to keep growing , and learning, and smiling,
because she would ...

Even though I miss her.

Today we went to the grave to visit.
Mom held my hand and said we could visit any time.

I liked that idea because I could talk to her in my head. It's not always easy to talk about her because I don't like crying or making others cry.

Today we went to the beach and played all day.
She would have liked that.
And the feel of the sunshine on her face.
We smiled as we made sandcastles.
And we felt like she was smiling down from heaven.

It's not easy to have a sister die.
There are good days and bad days.
There are times I remember her and laugh.
There are times I remember her and cry.

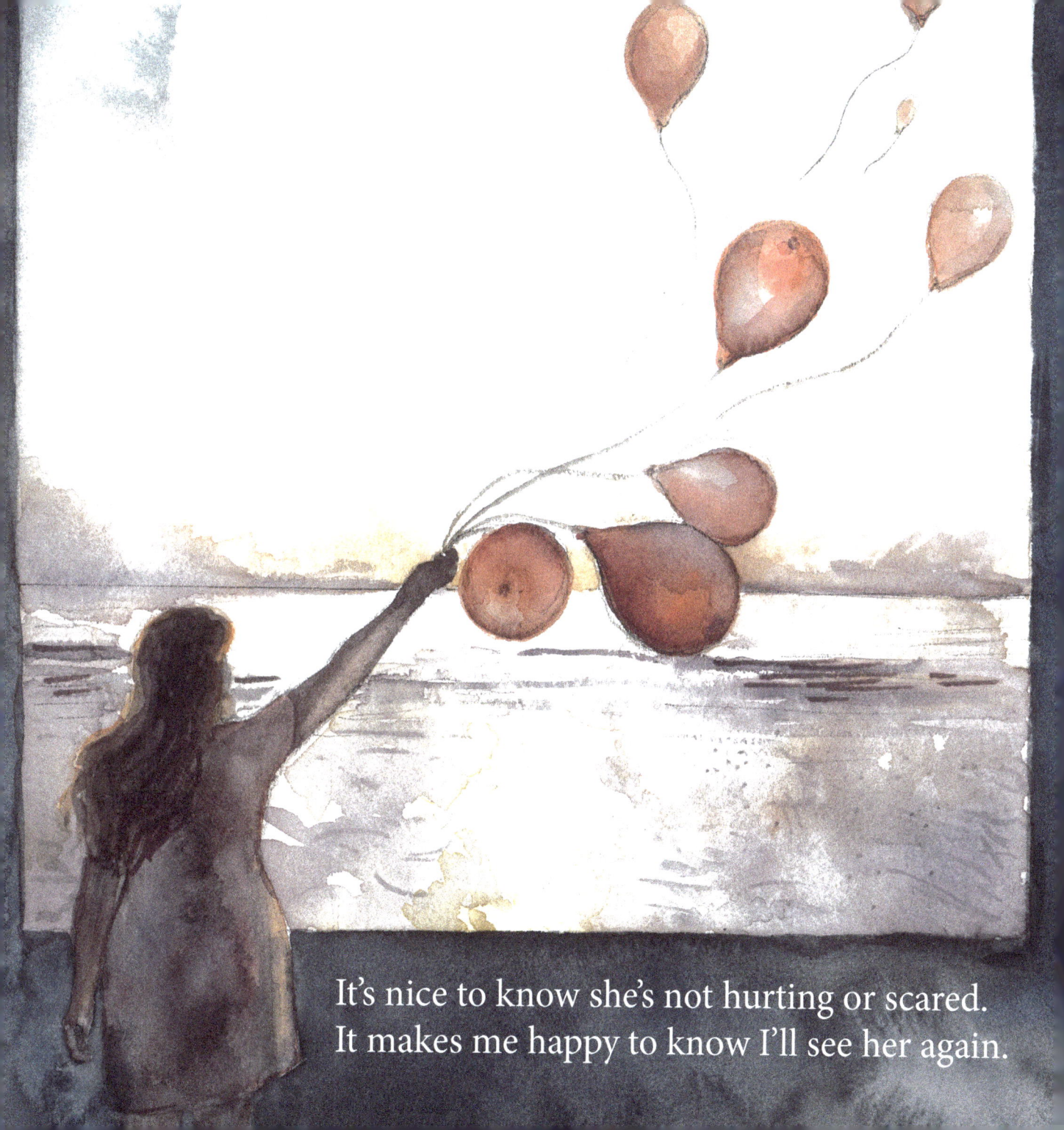

It's nice to know she's not hurting or scared.
It makes me happy to know I'll see her again.

I had a sister.
She was funny and strong and kind.

And today, I will be strong and funny and kind.

As I remember her and smile.

Other Resources:

Bereavedparentsusa.org

Compassionatefriends.org

Umbrellaministries.com

Remembering My Someone Special, Grieving Journal for Kids
(www.christianbook.com)

BASIS
(HVMI.org)

Joanneparkerbooks.com

Joanne Parker is a writer from West Chester, PA. After the death of her sister following a fatal car accident she decided to write a book about grief and loss to offer people hope and healing. When she's not running after one of her four children she keeps herself busy with music, theater, CrossFit, and local volunteering. She currently lives in Mobile, AL with her family and two dogs.

Sarah Posey is a freelance painter from Mobile, Alabama, currently pursuing an undergraduate degree in painting from the Savannah College of Art and Design. Besides "I Had a Sister," Sarah has dabbled in commissioned portraiture, graphic design, and has been shown in several local and regional fine art shows.

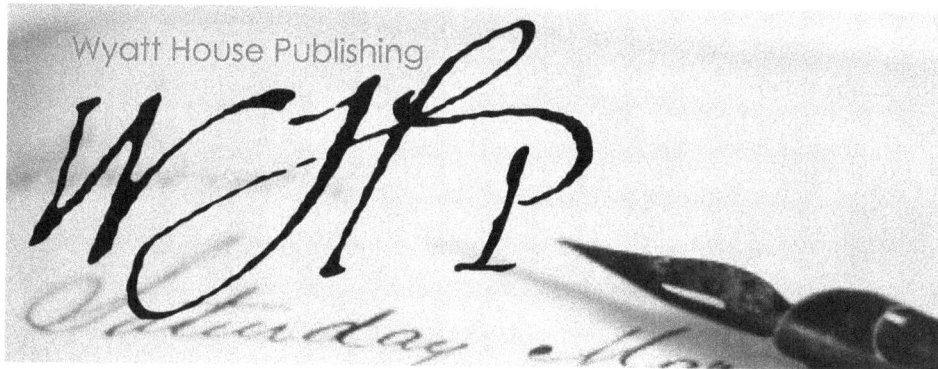

www.ingramcontent.com/pod-product-compliance
Lightning Source LLC
Chambersburg PA
CBHW081228040426
42445CB00016B/1920